Triumph Over Tragedy

The Life of
Edith Arendrup
A Victorian Courtauld

1846 - 1934

by

Richard Milward M.A.

ISBN 0-9501068-3-6

Produced by Merton Priory Press
Page makeup by Pippin DTP Services
Printed in England by Roebuck Press
Kingston Road, Merton, SW19 1LT

Contents

Illustrations

Acknowledgements

To Dame Gillian Brown and her sister, Mrs. Juliet Frankland, Edith's step great-granddaughters, to William E. Balars, to Sister Mary Cuthbert of the Franciscan Convent at Bocking and to the nuns' chaplain, Mgr. John Roche, for their invaluable help and encouragement with the writing of this biography.

To Aage Arendrup, great-nephew of Edith's husband, for kindly allowing me to use his wonderful collection of family letters.

To George Courtauld of Earl's Colne, Essex, and his brother, Simon, for their great interest in the project.

To Sister Cirilla de Freitas of Funchal, Madeira, for providing information about Edith's work on the island.

To my brother, John, Bill McGregor of the Sacred Heart parish, Wimbledon, and Norah Mitchell of the Daughters of the Heart of Mary who read the text and made valuable suggestions.

To Molly Cadie for typing the text.

Introduction - Who Was Edith Arendrup?

On Tuesday 30 January 1934 a Solemn Requiem was celebrated in the church of the Sacred Heart, Wimbledon. It was a very impressive ceremony – three priests vested in black at the altar, a large choir in the gallery at the west end, altar servers, one swinging a thurible from which incense curled up towards the roof, and in front of the altar rails a high catafalque, draped in black and flanked by six tall candlesticks.

The Requiem was a memorial Mass for 'the foundress of this church'. Over fifty years earlier and on her own initiative, she had started the parish and then provided most of the money to build its fine church. By now, however, few could remember her living in Wimbledon. Before the church had been finished, she had suddenly left the area and had since only returned to visit relatives and a few close friends. So by 1934 to most Wimbledon Catholics she was just a name: Madame Edith Arendrup.

A great deal of mystery surrounded her: What nationality was she, with the French title Madame, an English Christian name and a Danish surname? Who had she been before her marriage? How did she come to have so much money? What happened to her after the sudden disappearance from Wimbledon? To help answer these questions, the only source seemed to be a small pamphlet, *The Birth of a Mission*, based on her memories and published in 1926, but it provided no clues to the mystery. As years passed her memory faded and in 1968 when her only monument in the church, her private altar kept in the Sacred Heart Chapel, was destroyed to make way for a modern statue and altar, there was hardly a protest. It was not until 1977, as preparations were beginning to celebrate the centenary of the parish, that a serious attempt was made to discover who really was Edith Arendrup.

The first clues came, not through research in old documents, but in personal interviews. An old lady, whose memory had largely gone and who found it very difficult to concentrate on questions, provided the vital break-through. When asked who Edith Arendrup was before her marriage, her face brightened and she replied: 'Oh! Don't you know? She was a Courtauld'. Another elderly lady revealed that on leaving Wimbledon, Edith Arendrup had joined a religious order. Shortly afterwards a nun, living in the old Courtauld home in Essex which had since become a Franciscan Convent, wrote to say that Edith had retired there in old age and lay buried in its grounds. With this basic information, it was possible to begin the research needed to provide a brief outline of the life of the lady who had founded the parish in 1877.

This account, however, gave no real idea of her true personality. The clues for this did not come until ten years later in 1987, just after the church of the Sacred Heart had celebrated its centenary. A review of a short history of the church appeared in *The Tablet*, where an American reader recognised the name Arendrup and showed the article to Dame Gillian Brown, a step great-granddaughter of Edith Arendrup. She wrote to the parish priest and later sent a large collection of family photographs, documents and above all letters. The personal details contained in them gave much greater depth to the events of her life and a much clearer idea of her personality.

One final mystery remained: when, where and why did she become a Catholic? Lengthy research has produced a few hints towards an answer, but the problem is still unsolved. Nonetheless, even without the missing clues to the most important decision in her life, Edith Arendrup's biography seems well worth writing.

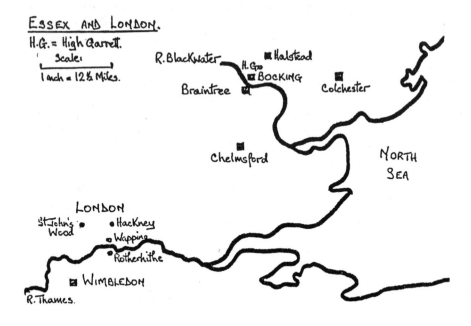

Essex and the London Area

1. Early Life

Madame Arendrup was born Edith Courtauld at Braintree, a small market-town in Essex, on 1 September 1846. Her father, John Minton Courtauld was in his late thirties and a junior partner in the family firm which made silk and crêpe. Her mother, Sarah Bromley, a daughter of another partner (and a Courtauld by descent), was in her early thirties. Edith was their second and last child; her brother Julien had been born two years earlier.

The Courtauld family were originally Huguenot refugees. They had come to England from the region of La Rochelle in Western France in 1686 and had settled in London as silversmiths. In 1801 Edith's grandfather, George Courtauld, set up a silk mill at Pebmarsh in Essex and eight years later established a second mill twelve miles away at Braintree. He does not seem, however, to have been an efficient businessman. In 1830 he left for America after handing control of the firm to his eldest son, Samuel, who had already set up on his own with a water-powered mill at Bocking, just north of Braintree. Under his strong and energetic direction, business revived, extra mills (all steam-powered) were built at Bocking and a new one making crêpe, the black material essential for Victorian funerals, was set up six miles further north at Halstead.

By the 1840s Samuel Courtauld and Co. were the leading employers in the Braintree area. They soon gained the reputation of treating their employees well. They rewarded good workers with bonuses; they built cottages, a school, a library and a club; in bad times, above all during the so-called 'Hungry Forties', they refused to sack any worker until there was no alternative. Just before Edith's birth, the partners were entertained to a massive dinner paid for by their employees who had set up a large marquee in front of Samuel's home, Folly House, High Garrett, on the main road linking Bocking and Halstead.

The Courtaulds were Unitarian in religion, serious-minded, and humanitarian in outlook. They lived in a strongly Nonconformist area, but were almost the only Unitarians. As a result, they attended chapel at Hackney in north London, until Samuel Courtauld, a very religious man, built a local chapel at High Garrett. They also always married fellow Unitarians. Edith's father and mother were both Unitarian and married at the chapel in Hackney in 1837.

Apparently they started life 'with limited means'. Edith's father was manager of one of the Bocking mills, but he seems often to have been ill and only became a junior partner under his older brother three years after Edith's birth. He was then able to buy a fine Regency house at Bocking Bridge, opposite a corn mill, with large grounds by the river Blackwater, an ideal place for young children.

Edith's early years seem to have been happy and untroubled. As the younger of the two children and the only girl, she was spoilt by her parents. In their letters she was referred to as 'Dear' or 'Our little dear', while she and Julien were 'the chicks'. They were regularly taken for holidays to Brighton or Scarborough. During one holiday in 1853, Edith (now seven) wrote to thank her Aunt Sophia for a silver pencil-case with E. engraved on it:

'Dear Aunt, I hope you are quite well. I like my pencil you gave me. Papa is better and getting up. I wish you were at Brighton. Where are you now? This morning a little cat jumped in at Mama's window and I caught it. Poor Julie is ill. I thank you for the pencil. Mama sends love. Good-bye from Dear. Miss Courtauld.'

Two years later when she was only nine, Edith suffered the first of many tragedies in her life: she lost her mother. Sarah Courtauld loved riding and most afternoons went out on her horse. One day in 1855 she left Bocking Bridge and galloped up the Halstead road towards High Garrett. For some reason the horse suddenly bolted and threw her out of the saddle. Tragically one of her feet got caught in the stirrup and she was dragged along the ground for nearly two miles. By the time the horse halted, she was dead. The sudden loss of their mother had a profound effect on both children, but especially on Edith. For a time they were looked after by their Aunt Sophia who became particularly fond of the little girl. She described her as 'melancholy and sweet...very intelligent in conversation and very observant...unselfish and interested in others'. She nicknamed her 'Little Abbess' as she wore a chain of black beads like a rosary round her neck and was very conscious of 'her own deep, lonely sorrow'.

After the death of her mother, Edith became even dearer to her father. She was taken on holidays abroad, to Nice and Italy. Above all, she was indulged in her greatest early ambition: to become an artist.

Bridge House, Bocking, Edith's Home.
Photographed in about 1890.

Edith and her brother, Julien.

5

Edith's Father, John Minton Courtauld.

Edith photographed in her early twenties.

6

2. Learning To Paint

Edith once described herself as 'an artist at heart' from her earliest childhood. Apparently no previous member of the Courtauld family had ever shown any artistic ability. Yet as a little girl she used to hide in the bushes in the big garden at Bocking Bridge and slowly declare: 'I am an artist'.

She seems to have been educated at home but instead of getting on with her sums, she used her slate to draw. She loved drawing, above all the horses in the family stables. Then in her early 'teens she was taught to paint in oil by an aunt (probably Catherine Hering, an artist) and soon produced her first original picture, *Late evening in a flat, marshy land, a sky of hurrying clouds, a sluggish river in the foreground and two large bullocks*. This was followed by two paintings of scenery in Scotland, the result of a family holiday. They were shown to the famous Victorian artist, Edwin Landseer, and won his praise. Unfortunately, he advised the young artist to go her own way and avoid all teaching.

Edith later said that the years 1861 to 1864, leading to her eighteenth birthday, were a period of 'hope and despair'. She described herself as 'dreamy and imaginative', but also 'rudderless'. Her father built her a studio in a field across a small road from their garden. There she painted enormous pictures, eight to ten feet long, of dramatic subjects such as *Dante's first entrance into Hell*, *The Destruction of Pharoah's host in the Red Sea* and *Man's Strife, God's Peace*, showing a battle-field after the cease-fire. She remembered that she 'worked madly or crouched in tears of despair'. The pictures were sent to the Royal Academy, but all were rejected, though one smaller work *Twilight* was accepted in 1864.

That year she finally decided that she needed some guidance. So she enrolled at the recently-founded National Art Training School in South Kensington. Under the direction of Richard Redgrave R.A., the first Keeper of Paintings at the future Victoria and Albert Museum, she learnt to draw from casts and for the first time studied anatomy. She also visited art galleries and made a lot of sketches. But she soon found the regular train journey from Braintree too much of a strain and left the Art School after only a term. Instead, she read Ruskin's *Modern Painters* (whose second volume had come out in 1846, the year of her birth); as a result, she gained 'a better idea of what was needed' and so, she felt, her painting improved. She also went abroad with her father and visited art galleries, especially in Paris and Milan.

The turning-point came in the autumn of 1866. For the past few months she had been working at a large painting, *Dawn: the Death of Moses*. She felt it was 'full of faults in the figures', but decided to bring it up to London and find some professional advice. Probably with the help of her uncle, George Hering, a landscape artist, she got an introduction to a leading Royal Academician, John Herbert, famous for his frescoes in the Peers' robing room at Westminster Palace. He was 'very kind' and gave her 'valuable advice'. In particular, he set her to study the human figure, which her father tried to stop as 'he did not want her to become a serious painter'. In the

7

Edith Arendrup's only picture still on display -- a milking scene painted in Madeira in the 1880s or early 1890s.

end, Mr. Courtauld not merely 'gave way to her entreaties,' but allowed her to use a small iron studio in her uncle's garden at the back of 45 Grove End Road, St. John's Wood.

Edith 'for the first time was in the company of artists'. Her work was 'overlooked' by John Herbert and also by another Academician, John Hodgson. Hodgson was a leading member of the so-called St. John's Wood Clique, a collection of young artists living in or near Grove End Road. Every Saturday they met in one or other of their homes to draw a given subject and then criticise each other's work (perhaps the best known of their many works is William Yeames's *And when did you last see your father?*). During the winter they all congregated in Hodgson's house and painted large frescoes all over the walls. So almost certainly Edith would have met these famous young men. She now spent alternate weeks at St. John's Wood and Braintree, and was 'very happy'. Her painting too began to improve. In 1868 one of her landscapes, *Wind and Cloud*, was accepted by the Royal Academy and hung at the Summer Exhibition.

Success made her more independent. In the autumn of 1870, now aged twenty-four, she rented her own house and studio in St. John's Wood at 35 Grove End Road and stayed there with a lady friend over the winter months. She did the same the next year. The result was a series of really talented paintings: *Memories of the first Palm Sunday*, exhibited at the Royal Academy in 1871 and bought by the National Gallery of Victoria, Melbourne, Australia, for £157.10s.; *Peter went out and wept bitterly* and *Daybreak on Mount Calvary*, hung at the Summer Exhibition of 1872; and *The Crown of Tribulation*, shown at the Royal Society of British Artists in 1873.

Then in the autumn of 1872 she went out to Egypt with her father. Her plan was to do more painting and to see Eastern scenery, light and colouring at first hand. Instead, she met Søoren Adolph Arendrup and married him the following summer. After settling down in Cairo, she returned to painting and produced a final large devotional picture, *Earth hath lost her King*, exhibited at the Academy in 1874. She then turned for inspiration to Egyptian scenes and in the next year three of her pictures, *On the Edge of the Desert*, *Sheep in the Desert: Sunset* and *Desert Well* were shown at the Royal Society of British Artists.

The sudden death of her husband and her return to England in 1876 seem to have ended her ambition to become a great artist. She had one last picture hung at the Royal Academy, *Nubian Captives in Egypt* (1878), and while on holiday in Madeira in the late 1880s or early 1890s she painted a huge and very striking canvas of a milking scene. Of all her pictures this is the only one still on show, in the Church Hall that she built for the Catholics of Halstead. *The First Palm Sunday* is now kept permanently in store in the National Gallery of Victoria; all the other paintings seem to have vanished. Her work as an artist is only mentioned in one reference book and her childish hopes of fame from her brush have proved vain.

3. Conversion To Catholicism

It was in the years when she was trying to establish herself as an artist that the real turning point in Edith's life occurred, her conversion to Catholicism. But the exact date and place of her reception into the Church are still mysteries, and only hints can be given for the reason behind her decision.

In 1897, on making her profession as a Daughter of the Heart of Mary, she declared that her conversion had taken place 'at the age of seventeen', in other words between 1863 and 1864. Unfortunately she provided no other information. Twenty years earlier, however, she seems to have left Elizabeth Clayton, author of *English Female Artists* (1875), with the impression that it had occurred several years later. She also seems to have suggested a motive. Mrs. Clayton wrote:

> 'At this time [about 1869] her mind was set at rest on a question by which it had long been agitated. She had been brought up in an atmosphere more resembling the higher and more moral side of the old Grecian philosophers than any Christian sect. By nature deeply devotional, the weary heart found rest within the Catholic Church.'

This discreet, general account of the conversion leaves many questions unanswered. It does not explain the factors that undermined her faith in the Courtauld family's Unitarianism. Above all, it makes no mention of the influences that led her towards Catholicism, a religion that had almost died out in Essex before 1870.

The first Catholics Edith ever met seem to have been among the London artists. John Herbert, a great influence on her paintings, was one. He had been converted through his friendship with Augustus Welby Pugin and Cardinal Wiseman, and had become a fervent Catholic, helping to found the St. Vincent de Paul Society in England to aid poor families. A far stronger influence, however, seems to have been the culture and religion of France.

Edith's ancestors had come from France and she herself learnt to speak French fluently. It is therefore possible that she had already stayed in the country to 'finish her education,' but her first known visit was with her father in 1865. She went primarily to study the paintings in the great art galleries in Paris, above all the Louvre. But she was clearly impressed by the country, then flourishing under the Second Empire of Napoleon III. In particular she saw Paris being transformed by its Prefect, Baron Haussmann, into a city of broad Boulevards, great Places and large Parks. She also arrived at a time when the French Church was in the middle of a great revival. Priests were said to be 'more youthful and dynamic'; new religious orders like the Marists were being founded; new churches were going up all over the country; devotion to the Sacred Heart was spreading (as was that to Our Lady of Lourdes after her apparitions were declared genuine in 1852); above all, Catholicism was still the religion of the majority of French men and women.

Such a cultured and religious atmosphere had a profound effect on Edith. In later years she returned to France over and over again; she even went to live in Paris for a number of years. She seems to have regarded France as her second home, hence her decision to be married there. So perhaps it was in France that she was received into the Catholic Church. The ceremony may even have taken place in the church in Paris (said to have been St. Pierre) where she was married in August 1873.

Wherever her conversion took place and whatever influenced her, there can be no doubt of its central importance for Edith. It changed her life. It also helped her to survive a second family tragedy, the sudden death of her brother.

Julien had recently taken over from his father as partner in the Courtauld silk business and had already shown 'shrewdness in business' and 'a happy, amiable disposition'. The day before his twenty-sixth birthday at the end of March 1870, he complained of feeling unwell and went to his room. What happened then was explained at the inquest. A family friend, Miss Matilda Hayes, told the coroner that just before 10p.m., 'Miss Courtauld rushed to the door of my room in an agitated state, exclaiming: "Oh, there is something dreadful the matter with Julien". At the same time she heard 'a howl like that of a dog' and thought it was Edith's dog at the door. But the noise was repeated and was followed by a groan. So, she took a candle, went into Julien's room and found him lying on his back in bed, his arms stretched out and his hands closed. At once she sent a messenger on horse-back for the doctor, but before he could arrive Julien was dead. Two Professors at London hospitals who conducted the post-mortem said that they had found prussic acid in his stomach and that this had stopped his heart. The cook gave evidence that he had gone twice to his 'photography room' that afternoon. In that room he would have used a solution of prussic acid as the developer for his photos. So the verdict of the inquest was that

> 'the deceased died from prussic acid, supposed to be administered by himself but under what circumstances there was no evidence to show, but to the best of their judgment and belief it was not taken for the purpose of destroying himself.'

Julien's sudden death seems to have led to the break-up of the family home. The autumn and winter of 1870 Edith spent at her new house and studio in London. At the same time her paintings were no longer of animals or landscapes, but of Palm Sunday and Christ's Passion. She was also becoming interested in the Near East.

4. Marriage And Life In Egypt

It was almost certainly a desire to see the lands of the Bible at first hand that led her in the autumn of 1872 to sail to the Eastern Mediterranean with her father in his yacht, the *Egidia*. She planned to spend the winter painting in Cairo. Instead, she met a Danish officer, Lieutenant-Colonel Arendrup.

Søren Adolph Arendrup was a member of a well known family in Denmark. His father was a distinguished doctor; one of his younger brothers became Governor of the Danish West Indies, the other a Major-General in the Danish Army. He too joined the Army and was described as 'exceptionally gifted' as an artillery officer. In 1860 when he was twenty-six he married the daughter of a Danish Vice-Admiral (like Edith, of Huguenot descent). They had two children, Harriet born in 1861, and Ebba born three years later. In 1868, however, his young wife died of tuberculosis and the doctors feared he also had the disease. So they recommended him to stay in the warm, dry climate of Egypt. There he became friendly with General Stone, an American officer who was reorganising the army for the Khedive. The general was impressed with his 'high intelligence, honorable bearing and evident knowledge of his profession' and offered him the post of Lieutenant-Colonel in the Egyptian army. As chances of promotion at home were then poor, he accepted and soon was promoted Adjutant to the Khedive.

Edith was strongly attracted by this distinguished officer. He was now aged thirty-eight, thirteen years older than herself, and a widower with two little girls, but he was tall, handsome and a true gentleman. She too was attractive, so they soon became engaged and arranged to marry in the following summer of 1873. Meanwhile, Adolph (as she called him) travelled back to Denmark to tell his family, while Edith and her father returned home.

The civil marriage took place at Marylebone Registry Office on 27 August. On the marriage certificate Adolph described himself as 'aged 39; widower; Lieutenant-Colonel Egyptian Army'; Edith as 'aged 26; spinster; no profession'. The witnesses were her father and Mr. and Mrs. MacCallum, friends they had made in Egypt. As soon as the ceremony was over, they boarded a train for Dover, crossed the Channel (described that day as 'rather rough') and went to Paris. There on the next day, 28 August, the religious ceremony took place in church before a Catholic priest. Adolph was a Lutheran and so there could be no nuptial Mass, but at least they had the Church's blessing.

Husband and wife spent part of their honeymoon at Fontainebleau. From the Hotel de Lyons Edith wrote for the first time to her little step-daughters, Harriet (Hattie) and Ebba, in Denmark:

> 'My two little darlings. Although you do not know me yet, I cannot help writing these few words to you to send you love and kisses. Do you think it is funny that I should love two little girls whom I have never

Colonel Sven Adolf Arendrup.

Edith's first letter to her step-daughters.

seen? Well, never mind. I will not ask as much from you, but only that you will give me your love. When I come to Denmark, we shall all three have to teach each other, though I am not sure I shall find I have to teach you much English, but you will certainly have to teach me Danish! I hope the two dolls are quite well. Pray tell them I hope they thank me for giving them such good little mothers.'

Adolph and Edith then returned to England. In October they crossed to Denmark and visited the Arendrup family home in Denmark. A few months later Edith mentioned one very moving incident during the visit in another letter to Harriet:

'How well I remember the morning we visited together your mother's grave. I am glad it looks so beautiful now. That was a sad morning and as we stood by the grave, I longed so much to be able to comfort you a little for the loss of that sweet mother. You know I lost my dear mother when I was very young and know so well what a loss it is. When we are together, dear Harriet, you will tell me a great deal about her, will you my darling? and I will tell you of mine. I believe the spirits of both are ever near us and I believe your dear mother's spirit will help me to be of some comfort to you.'

Husband and wife then settled in Egypt. Adolph's headquarters was in the Abbassieh barracks, Cairo. So their home was almost certainly in the suburb of

15

Heliopolis, where most Europeans lived and where Edith probably adopted the form of address used in Cairo expatriate society, 'Madame Arendrup'. There in June 1874 was born their first child, a girl soon christened Agnes. Edith was clearly delighted and wrote to 'my darling little Ebba,' then just ten, to tell her of 'the new little sister':

> 'She is such a tiny little thing; you could nurse her like a doll – indeed I do not think she is much bigger than your doll Edith.'

Sadly the baby only survived two months in the Egyptian heat. She died on 19 August, leaving her parents heart-broken. But they had little time to mourn their loss as early in September Adolph was promoted Colonel and given command of an Egyptian Army to attack Ethiopia.

The two countries had a long-standing border dispute. The Khedive hoped to make the Emperor of Ethiopia give way by sending a force of 2,500 men, armed with the latest Remington rifles and two six-gun batteries of mountain howitzers. They went by sea to Massawa (now in Eritrea) and marched into the interior towards Asmara. For ten days all went well, but on 17 November 1875 at Gundet on the river Mareb they found themselves faced with the entire Ethiopian Army (variously estimated between 10, and 70,000 men), led by the Emperor, who had an English General as his Chief of Staff. The Ethiopian weapons were inferior to the Egyptian, but their morale was high and they were defending their country against hated invaders. The fighting was severe and the Egyptians were forced to retreat. Then

Colonel Arendrup, who had led his men with great bravery, was shot and killed. Egyptian resistance disintegrated and the force was cut to pieces. Four days later a Frenchman visited the battlefield and saw Adolph's body:

> 'His wound was through the ear into the brain and death must have been instantaneous. He was lying face upwards with a smile on his lips. His clothes had not been disturbed, but all his possessions – watch, rings etc. – had gone.'

General Gordon later reported that the grave had been marked by a great heap of stones and 'is known and respected by the whole country'. *The Times*, mentioning the death, reported that 'Colonel Arendrup was a very popular man; his high moral and intellectual character had won the esteem of the European community, and his fine soldierly figure and pleasant face will be greatly missed at many a house in Cairo'.

Edith was shattered when the news reached her. She had already lost her mother and her only brother by sudden death. Now within a few months she had also lost her baby daughter and her husband. Only her religion – and Adolph's memory – saved her from a complete breakdown. She was expecting another baby. It was born two months later, in January 1876, and the proud mother promptly wrote from Cairo to tell Harriet:

> 'My darling! I must send you a few lines to tell you our baby is born and is a great big, fat, splendid boy. Are you not glad, darling? Both he and your mother are quite well and getting on nicely. You cannot think what a big, beautiful fellow he is; everyone says he is more like a baby of two months old. He will be like Father, I am sure.'

The baby was christened Axel Jerome. The choice was explained by Edith to her mother-in-law in Denmark:

> 'Dear Adolph always wished our son named Axel if we ever had one. I pray God he may grow up as noble and good as his father.'

Mother and baby clearly could not remain in Egypt. So very reluctantly Edith decided to return home in the spring with a Danish lady friend. Just before she left, she wrote again to her mother-in-law, expressing her fears for the future:

> 'It makes me very sad to think of going away from this sweet home which has held all that was dearest to me on earth, and where I have been so blessed and so happy. It makes me shrink to think of going out from its sheltering walls and beginning a new life – a life that must ever be a maimed and lonely one – for even with the blessing that God gives me in my children, no children can fill the place of my beloved husband. But I will not be a coward. Adolph shall never feel that he has a cowardly wife who shrinks from carrying her cross bravely.'

WINDOW & GROVE   63ᴬ BAKER STREET, W.

Edith, the young widow photographed
shortly after leaving Egypt in 1876.

18

5. A New Home In Wimbledon

Edith Arendrup had left England in the summer of 1873 as a young bride of twenty-six, looking forward to life in Egypt. Now less than three years later she returned a sorrowing widow with a tiny baby and an uncertain future. She was met by her father and taken to their old home at Braintree. There she was able to settle down again to life in England and to decide what was best for herself and for the baby. Axel was a sickly child and needed both country air and the availability of a good doctor. Bridge House, Bocking was not ideal for such needs and anyway her father was planning to marry again – his own sister-in-law, which was then illegal in England and meant a move abroad. So he offered to buy his daughter a house.

The district they finally chose was the new garden suburb of Cottenham Park, Wimbledon. Until 1851 it had been a large country estate, owned by the Lord Chancellor, Charles Pepys, Earl of Cottenham. On his death the land had been sold for development, but twenty-five years later few houses had been built except along the one main road in the area, Copse Hill. There Edith's aunt Ellen and her husband, Charles Knowlys Grenside, a solicitor, had bought an acre of land in 1857 and had had a house built which they called Oakfield. When they first came to Cottenham Park they felt very isolated. So Charles bought a swordstick as a protection during the long walk from Wimbledon Station on dark winter nights, while Ellen was given a revolver and practised firing at a box in the garden. Yet now twenty years later conditions had so improved that they could suggest to Edith that she should follow their example and settle there.

The house she chose was one of three just built by the side of an old carriage drive, now known as Cottenham Park Road. Edith described it as 'this charming little house'. It still stands, though divided into flats and called Barkby Close. It certainly is an impressive Victorian building with its dark red brick, large windows, unusual chimneys and fleur-de-lis decoration in plaster across the front. But by no stretch of the imagination could it be described as 'little'. It has two very large rooms opening off the hall downstairs and two more on the first floor, with a fine view towards Epsom Downs. It also has an annexe which used to contain a stable for the horse, Meg, and the carriage. Beyond, there was a triangular garden with a large summer house, now covered by three modern houses.

Edith and Axel, now one year old, moved in early in 1877. She called the house 'The Abbassieh' to remind her of her husband's headquarters in Cairo. Soon her two step-daughters, Harriet and Ebba, came to live with her. They were looked after by three servants, an Irish woman, Hannah Dwyer, and two Londoners, Lilly Lambert and Amy Fuller. So she was now able to entertain friends. She held 'At Homes' and gave dinner parties, to one of which she invited four young Courtauld nieces, boarders at Donhead House, a 'Ladies' School' run by Miss Arnold in Edge Hill. As well as the horse, she owned a dog, perhaps for security as policemen were still rarely seen in Cottenham Park. To judge from her letters, she never seems to have been

19

Map: Wimbledon in 1913. Scale 1:2500.
Reproduced from the 1913 Ordnance
Survey Map.

B = Barkby Close
O = Oakfield

burgled; in fact the only occasion she mentions any concern over the house was during 'terrific gales' at some time in the early 1880s (Edith had an infuriating habit of rarely dating any of her letters):

'I have been literally kept awake by the roaring and howling of the wind, and expecting every minute to hear the chimneys blown down.'

Not long after settling in Cottenham Park, she received a far worse shock. Less than a month after remarrying in Switzerland, her father suddenly died. Over the years and particularly since her brother's sad death, they had been very close and so Edith felt this new tragedy in her life deeply. Apart from her baby son and her young step-daughters, she was alone. She inherited a large share of her father's fortune which was said to be about £100,000, and so had no worries about money. But she now had to take complete charge of her family without any father or husband to help her.

She sent both her step-daughters to an English school, Cheltenham Ladies' College, where Ebba, the younger girl, did particularly well, finishing first in class. Harriet, on the other hand, disliked Cheltenham and found it harder to adapt to life in England. In one letter Edith told her bluntly: 'I can't help thinking you'd be happier if you got into the habit of talking to me more.' Yet she still sent her ' lots and lots of love and kisses from your own Mammie.' The girls in fact, though very different in temperament, were both devoted to her, and both made excellent marriages. Ebba married her cousin, Major General Albert Arendrup, settled in Denmark, had four children and kept up a long and affectionate correspondence with her step-mother. Harriet married her step-mother's first cousin, Charles Evelyn Grenside, the only son of the family who had persuaded Edith to buy the house in Cottenham Park and whose garden hedge was just opposite The Abbassieh. They were married at St. Mary's Parish Church, Wimbledon, in March 1883 and, as the local paper reported, 'the party afterwards adjourned to Madame Arendrup's to partake of luncheon'. Harriet too had four children, one (Gerda) a talented artist. She often invited her step-mother to Oakfield after she had left The Abbassieh for good.

Edith's chief concern, however, was with her son. Axel (or 'Pax' as she called him) was clearly the apple of her eye and her letters were full of his doings. When he was only three 'he makes a great noise in the house now and likes to look out of the window and call out to everyone who passes.' Later while staying with Courtauld relatives in Essex, 'he hunts with a small musket in the woods and goes in a boat on the lake.' But his chief delight seems to have been the family horse Meg: 'Axel is getting to ride quite nicely and can trot without being held.' Unfortunately the animal could be 'quite wild – kicked and jumped and galloped like mad.' In July 1887, shortly after the opening of the Sacred Heart Church, it nearly killed Edith, just as another horse had caused the death of her mother thirty-two years before. The parish priest, Fr. Kerr, reported that 'Madame Arendrup was all but killed this morning in trying to save her boy from being run away with in her pony chaise.' He feared that she

Ebba, aged sixteen in 1880.

Harriet, aged fourteen in 1875.

would not survive that night and anointed her, but almost miraculously she recovered and a month later he was able to write in his journal 'Deo gratias'.

By then Edith was far more concerned over her son's health than over her own. Axel had never been strong and as he grew up he seemed ever more susceptible to illness. In 1884 she reluctantly sent him to Hodder, the preparatory school for Stonyhurst in Lancashire. After he had been there three weeks, she wrote to 'Dearest Aboo' (Axel's name for Ebba):

> 'I am so glad that Pax is at last settling down very happily at school – and the worst is over for both of us, I hope – if only he keeps well. He enjoys the cricket and is getting quite school-boyish. He fought a boy the other day and beat him – "but he was smaller than me, Mammie." The boys all seem to like him and treat him much more gently than they do each other. Fr. Cassidy says he doesn't know why (of course, I think it's because he is so sweet!)'.

Unfortunately only a few days later he had an attack of 'hay asthma'. Edith had to remove him from school and take him to Blackpool where he soon recovered. From then on he seems to have had private lessons at home. By 1892 he was certainly 'busy doing lessons – six hours a day – to try and pass matriculation at London University.' He had set his heart on going into the Navy. He did in fact pass the exam for a Cadetship and served for a time on the training-ship 'Britannia' (with two medallions of the Sacred Heart sewed into his uniform by his anxious mother). In the end his health proved too delicate and Edith wrote to her mother-in-law:

> 'You know he has had to give up the Navy – it is a great disappointment, but cannot be helped. Thank God, he is much better now [probably 1894] and I hope in a few years he may yet be a sufficiently strong man to live a happy and useful life. He intends now to devote himself to Science – Zoology – of which he is passionately fond and I hope he will make a good position for himself in this way.'

To help restore his health, Edith took Axel to Madeira or Teneriffe almost every winter from the early 1880s. In Madeira he was looked after by an English nurse, Mary Jane Wilson (like Edith, a convert), who later started schools, an orphanage and a hospital on the island and founded the Congregation of Franciscan Sisters of Our Lady of Victories to run her institutions. Edith became her life-long friend. On every visit she brought Mary Jane tea and sausages which could not be obtained locally. She also gave money for a new ward in the hospital and for the building of a chapel and school, which is still known as the Arendrup School.

Axel seemed to flourish in the warmth of Madeira. In one letter written probably in the early 1890s, Edith told her step-daughter Ebba:

> 'Pax is tremendously busy making drawings of the lots of strange fish here. He goes to the fish-market every morning about 6.30, a walk of

Edith and Axel, aged six in 1882.

three miles there and back, and generally about four times a week finds some new fish and brings it home and draws it. All this of course has to be done between lesson hours and riding (which last I insist upon or he would be drawing all day!). We are enjoying Madeira very much, though it is not quite so nice as Teneriffe. About once or twice a month Axel has a whole holiday and we go long excursions, riding up into the mountains, lonely wild places.'

Just before Christmas 1894 he suddenly became ill and had to be sent off to Madeira 'at a moment's notice' with one of the servants. Edith followed a week later, but found that her ship did not stop at the island. So she had to write to Axel who was clearly much better and 'tell him to come to Teneriffe by himself – and I think he will rather enjoy the independence of managing for himself'.

This holiday was their last happy one. When they returned to Madeira for the winter of 1895-96 Axel became very seriously ill. First he had a bad attack of rheumatic fever, from which he had suffered before. He then contracted typhoid. His weak constitution could not fight the disease and on Easter Sunday 1896 he died. He was only just twenty.

The poor mother had to face the crowning tragedy. Already deprived of her mother, only brother, daughter, husband and father by sudden death, she now lost her only son. She buried him in Madeira with a simple stone cross over the grave and the word 'Pax' inscribed in large capital letters in the middle of the cross. Years later while staying in Rome, she wrote to Ebba:

'Easter always seems full of the thought of our darling Pax. And it is always in Heaven's light that I think of him, never in connexion with the sad time of illness that came first. The joy of the Resurrection seems to have wiped all that away.'

Bankby Close
Cottenham Park

Dec. '87.

The Abbassieh, Cottenham Park. drawn by
John Wallace about 1987.

6. Building The Sacred Heart Church

Edith Arendrup was not content just to manage her house in Cottenham Park and look after her family. As a recent convert to Catholicism, she was determined to try and spread her new Faith. A friend had advised her to 'open a chapel in one of your rooms and trust to God for the rest; you will see it will be the beginning of a big mission'.

In 1877 such a transformation seemed impossible. Wimbledon was a strongly Protestant suburb with a flourishing Evangelical movement, which was hostile to any semblance of 'Popery'. The first Catholic chapel in the area since the Reformation (in the grounds of the Keir on Westside) had been closed over twenty-five years earlier and the nearest Mass centre was four miles away across the Common at Roehampton. As a result, very few Catholics came to live in Wimbledon.

Edith set out to change this state of affairs. At first on Sundays she drove in her carriage to St. Joseph's church, Roehampton, to attend Mass. There she met the Jesuits who were running the parish, above all Fr. John Morris. Fr. Morris was a distinguished convert who had been private secretary to both Cardinal Wiseman and Cardinal Manning before joining the Jesuits. He then became the chief promoter of the cause of the English Martyrs, a well-known giver of retreats and a wise confessor. Edith soon took him as her own confessor and came to place great reliance on his judgment. 'When I placed myself under the direction of Fr. Morris,' she later said, 'there began a complete new birth in my spiritual life.'

Fr. Morris quickly realised that Edith 'wanted to do great work for God and that she was capable of carrying it out'. So he did all in his power to help her. He persuaded the Jesuit Rector at Roehampton to agree to send a priest to say Mass in her house, on condition that she provided a suitable chapel and got the approval of James Danell, the Bishop of Southwark. The chapel, a room by the entrance hall, she equipped with a small wooden altar, some candles and a few seats. The Bishop she approached through a letter written in August 1877:

> 'I take the liberty of addressing your Lordship to lay before you the great want of a church felt by myself and all the Catholics of Wimbledon. I therefore ask your Lordship's permission to have a chapel in my house until better accommodation can be offered. I have a room which with a slight alteration would be well fitted for such a purpose and I am willing to devote it to this and to throw it open to the public if your Lordship will give permission for it to be served from Roehampton.'

Edith followed the letter with a personal call at Bishop's House. On her visiting card the Bishop wrote: 'Leave given for private chapel.' The chapel was dedicated to Saints Jerome and Agnes (the names of her two children) and the first Mass was said there on Sunday, 2 December, 1877. The congregation was tiny; Edith, her

Fr John Morris S.J.

servants, two old Irish women who had previously walked all the way to Clapham on a Sunday, an Irish coachman and a French family who had fled to England after the Paris Commune. Edith commented that they were so few they could easily have taken tea together. Two years later a Jesuit reported that 'Catholicism at present makes little way in Wimbledon; it is regarded as the private concern of a few'.

Soon, however, numbers began to increase. By 1880 the room was said to be 'inconveniently crowded' and so Edith had a special chapel built on to the side of the house. It had Gothic windows, niches for statues of the two patron saints and a marble altar (the building survives, though used for very different purposes). But Edith was not satisfied. She asked the Bishop to provide a resident priest and promised to help with his maintenance. A secular priest was expected, but none came. Instead, she got the Bishop's permission to buy a plot of land in Russell Road in the heart of the working-class area of 'New Wimbledon' and there built a small elementary school with an iron chapel attached where Mass was also said on Sundays for the more numerous Catholics living either side of the Broadway. The size of the congregations at the two chapels continued to grow: In 1884, 400; 1885, 450; 1886, 550.

Edith realised that the only solution was to build a church. She wanted a large, beautiful building on a commanding site to proclaim to the whole district that the Catholic Church had returned to Wimbledon. By sheer chance the ideal site came on the market in the early 1880s: building plots 'on the north-west of an intended new road (called Darlaston Road)', being developed on the side of a hill above the fields along Worple Road. Acting through a solicitor, Frederick Stacey, she bought first two of the plots and then two more. On the recommendation of Fr. Morris, she chose a relatively unknown architect, Frederick Walters, who had designed the Jesuit church at Roehampton. Edith had several changes made to his original plans – a more decorated exterior, a large tower at the western end and a stone baldachino over the high altar. She also insisted that the church should be dedicated to the Sacred Heart and, looking to the future, that it should be capable of seating 800, nearly double the number of Catholics in 1885.

The nave of the new church was built in less than a year, at a cost of £8,000, all paid by Edith Arendrup. Sadly she could not attend the opening by Bishop Butt on the feast of the Sacred Heart, 17 June 1887, 'because of the serious illness of her child'. But she and Axel regularly attended services there, even though Mass was still said from time to time in her private chapel by Fr. Kerr, the first parish priest and a great friend. The Jesuit Journal records many gifts from her: a new carpet for the sanctuary, a candle-stand for the new statue of Our Lady, prayer books for the first communicants, as well as a turkey at Christmas for the priests and a day-out for the Russell Road school-children at her house. She also regularly 'decorated the pulpit and font' at Christmas, decorated the altar for the Forty Hours' exposition and arranged a Good Friday choral service with the organist in 1890. 'Master Axel Arendrup' carried the cross in one procession and in August 1891 made 'a communion of thanksgiving' on his recovery from rheumatic fever.

From the 7th S. in Advent?

CHAPEL OF

S.S. Jerome and Agnes,

THE ABBASSIEH,

COTTENHAM PARK ROAD, WIMBLEDON.

MASS on Sundays and Holidays at Nine o'clock.

CONFESSIONS before Mass at Half-past Eight.

The Collections at Mass will be for the Priest.

*Notice of the first Mass at The Abbassieh;
1st Sunday in Advent, December 1877.*

Three years later Edith told her step-daughter Ebba: 'I am beginning another piece of the church this summer'. This was the sanctuary and the apse. Both involved costly additions to the original plan: an extra bay to the sanctuary to accommodate the choir and three chapels opening off the apse to enable the extra Jesuit priests at the new College to say Mass in the mornings. Even Edith's purse was stretched by the considerable extra cost. So she had to ask two other wealthy ladies, Miss Fullerton and Mrs. Currie, 'to do' (as she put it) the two aisles. By 1901, however, she was in a position to complete the church with a fine west front looking onto Edge Hill. She had to give up the idea of a large bell tower; instead there were two smaller towers flanking a great west window. All these works cost her approximately £10,000 on top of the £8,000 for the nave. So in modern terms she spent about £800,000 for the building of one of the finest churches in the Wimbledon area. It is not surprising in the prevailing climate of opinion that this gift of Courtauld money for the Catholic cause shocked some of her relatives. That their views did not deter her illustrates her great strength of will.

Yet for Edith a far greater achievement was to have that church looked after by priests of the Society of Jesus. From the moment she first met the Jesuits at Roehampton, she was determined that they alone should be responsible for 'the Wimbledon mission'. But she had a very difficult task to persuade the Jesuit Provincial to support her plan. He was willing to allow a priest to go to Cottenham Park and Russell Road every Sunday and say Mass, but he had no desire to take on the permanent running of another parish so near Roehampton and politely declined her offer. Edith was bitterly disappointed, as she showed in a frank letter to the Bishop:

> 'If I had known that the mission could never belong to the Society, I should have purchased the land in a poorer neighbourhood and built a smaller and inexpensive chapel, which had been in better accordance with the prospects of the mission.'

Reluctantly she offered the church to the Bishop. But the secular clergy showed even less enthusiasm for it than the Jesuits. One priest died immediately after being appointed to take charge. Another asked to be sent to a larger place as he claimed he would die of boredom 'in such a God-forsaken hole'. Finally in March 1887, with the opening of the church only a few months away, a solution was found. The Bishop agreed to allow the Jesuits to open a day school in Wimbledon and the Provincial accepted charge of the mission. Edith was delighted, as she showed in a letter to the Provincial:

> 'I can scarcely realise that the mission I have fostered like a child for so long and my attempts for whose settlement have hitherto been invariably frustrated, should at last be so happily settled for life and in the way which of all others I have most desired. That it may prove a source of good fruit to the Society and not an unprofitable burden is now my great hope.'

Drawing of the Church by the architect.

The Church as it is today.

Over the past century her hopes, not simply for the Jesuits, but also for the Catholic Church in Wimbledon have been more than realised. When she arrived at Cottenham Park in 1877, Wimbledon had been regarded as 'a stronghold of Protestantism' with hardly a Catholic to be found. A mere twenty years later when she sold her house and left the district, it was being talked of as 'a hot-bed of Jesuit Popery' with an estimated 1,600 Catholics, numbers only surpassed by the Anglicans and the Baptists. The phenomenal growth was not simply due to the existence of a fine, large church, but to the opening in 1892 of the Jesuit College (for whose purchase Edith loaned the Society £4,000), followed by the Ursuline Convent. Both these schools drew many young middle-class parents to the area of Edge Hill. As a result, Catholics could no longer be treated as 'potential subversives out to enslave the minds' of good Protestants, but as normal members of the community fit to play their part in the life of the Borough. In 1910 extreme Protestants staged the last protest against the return of Catholicism to the area - a near riot against a procession up Edge Hill. The next year a Catholic was elected Mayor. Edith Arendrup had indeed inspired one of the most dramatic changes in the history of Wimbledon.

The chapel of the Sacred Heart, showing the original altar from Cottenham Park (since destroyed).

7. Work As A Religious

Edith's departure from Wimbledon in 1896 soon after the death of her son was not the sudden decision of a sorrowing mother. Had Axel lived another year, come of age and established himself in a suitable job, she would certainly have come to the same decision. Under the guidance of her confessor, Fr. Morris, she had learnt to 'be ready to strip herself of all possessions and abandon her whole life to Jesus'. In 1893, when Fr. Morris suddenly collapsed and died before her eyes while preaching in the Sacred Heart church, she found 'a truly sympathetic confidante and spiritual helper in a lady whom she had met in Paris'. This lady was a member of a religious institute, the Daughters of the Heart of Mary. Founded at the time of the French Revolution, the members do not wear any distinctive dress, nor do they necessarily live together in community. Instead they live a religious life either at home or in a mother house and carry on an active life 'in the world'. They are thus ready to undertake any kind of service where it is most needed. Such an apostolate, inspired by the ideas of St. Ignatius, immediately appealed to Edith and in 1895 she began 'her formation' in the institute while her son was still alive. His death the following year only hastened the decision to leave Wimbledon.

Before selling her house in Cottenham Park, she dismantled the chapel. The vestments, chalice and some religious paintings of her own (which have since disappeared) were given to the Sacred Heart church, as was the fine marble altar. It was installed in the middle chapel of the apse which was dedicated to the Sacred Heart of Jesus, 'the guiding star of her life'. On either side of the altar large stained glass windows with pictures of her favourite saints were 'erected by the congregation' in memory of Axel (who was shown kneeling in prayer in the bottom panel of the left-hand window) and 'as an offering to his mother'. Sadly the altar was broken up in 1968 when a modern altar and statue were installed, but the windows fortunately survive as a memorial to Edith's devotion to the Catholic Church in Wimbledon.

Once she was free of her commitments in England, she crossed the Channel to France. In February 1897, at the headquarters of the Daughters of the Heart of Mary in Paris, she took religious vows. For the next few years her movements are uncertain, but early in the new century she returned to London and went to see Cardinal Vaughan, the Archbishop of Westminster, probably an old friend. She asked how best she could serve the Church and at his suggestion decided to settle in Wapping in the heart of the London Docks, on the north side of the Thames. The area was full of poor immigrants, especially from Ireland, who lived in squalid, overcrowded tenements and worked long hours (if work was available) for very low pay. There were also many starving and abandoned children and, along the Ratcliff Highway, brothels, opium dens and drinking houses. It was a district to turn the stomachs of the most experienced social workers. Yet it was here that Edith, after 56 years spent in totally different surroundings, started her new 'unlady-like' work, much to the disapproval of a number of her relatives.

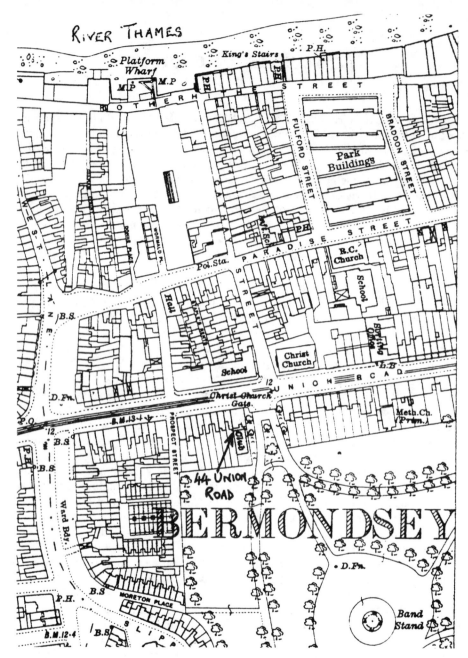

Map: Bermondsey and Rotherhithe about
1910, showing Edith's headquarters, 44
Union Road .

Some time in 1902 she settled in a large workmen's tenement, 18 New Tower Buildings, Wapping, which commanded a fine view of the Thames. She started the day whenever possible by going onto the flat roof to pray, then usually heard two Masses and placed herself at the disposal of the parish priest. On his behalf she visited every Catholic family in the district, organised a youth club and founded a Society of Nazareth for older women. The youth club met every evening. Edith provided papers and books, taught girls sewing, took parties on excursions and even organised football matches. For the older women, with whom naturally she 'was more at home', there were discussions on religion and on 'practical matters' every Sunday. In 1903 another Daughter of the Heart of Mary, Miss Elliot, came to help her, but the main burden still fell on her shoulders. Yet in letters to Ebba, she gave no hint of what she was doing, except once to say: 'I can so seldom get down to see Hatty ', her other step-daughter, Harriet, in Wimbledon.

In 1904 she was made Superior of the Daughters of the Heart of Mary house in Dublin, though she confided to Ebba:'I must say I'd rather be in England'. The Institute ran retreats, a Sunday School and classes for 'teenage girls. But Edith felt the house was too like a convent and handed it over to an order of nuns, despite opposition from some of the community. She then returned to the work she loved – among the poor in the Dublin slums. She visited the sick, organised a savings fund, held evening classes and clubs, including one for girl flower-sellers, and prepared children for their first Communion. The clubs did not go well and in their place she set up a house for young girls coming to Dublin from the country to find work. This proved a great success.

After spending eight years in Ireland, she returned to London and at last gave herself a real holiday. She travelled to Denmark to visit Ebba and her family with 'a warm heart full of love for you all'. Nothing is recorded about the stay, but the return journey was eventful:

> 'At Kiel,' Edith reported, 'I got some bread and cheese, and ensconced myself in the compartment for "Fruen", thinking to be free from German smokers who smoke everywhere. Two German ladies were there, much bedizened with jewels and so fat they made a straight line from their ample bosoms to their toes. No sooner started than they began to smoke and to talk without ceasing. They got into an animated discussion as to whether New York was in England or America! They finally appealed to me!! They got out at Ancona, shaking hands effusively with me! The sea passage was very rough. At Queenborough I was hedged in with five Germans, men and women, who smoked, though it wasn't a smoking carriage, all the way to London – and drank wine and laughed voraciously – and sat with arms round each other's waists. My politics got more hotly pronounced, even than before!!'

Immediately on her return she went back to Dockland. This time she settled near the Surrey Docks at 44 Union Road, Rotherhithe (the house is still there, though

① 44 Union Road
Rotherhithe
August 25

Iyland Also

I have been hesitating long about coming to Denmark — & I'm afraid I don't feel up to it. Whether it is the great heat we have been enduring for so long, or whether it is that I am really an *old* woman now, I don't know, — but I don't feel as if I could face the long journey. Perhaps

② next year, if we are not half killed by such abnormal heat I shall be better able for the journey.

Thank you, darling, for your kind letter. I hope you & Otto & Axel have been enjoying your fortnight near Albert. What is Otto doing now? Has he been able to begin his actual forest work or is he still having to

③ do a lot of studying. I hope Axel will work hard, & so be able to perpetuate the Arendrup military history with honour.

You will have been reading probably of our dreadful strike. It is quieted down now for the moment, except in Wales — but I think it is only the beginning of a sort of mob rule of

④ terrorism & revolution which is the natural outcome of the Socialistic spirit which is every where now. I am afraid that is the real spirit of the country — all the to-do of the Coronation, the Prince of Wales' Investiture etc is the skin-deep varnish.

You are a dear to think about my birthday. I'm too old to have birthdays now! What I should like very much is a good strong bag for my linen — with "Arendrup" big on it.

Letter from Edith to her step-daughter, Ebba, written in 1912.

38

now a shop and in Jamaica Road). The area was rather more pleasant than Wapping with a large park just behind the house and the Catholic church nearby, but its problems were very similar to those Edith had faced on the opposite side of the river. She ran St. Margaret's Centre, a hall just behind the house where every morning 250 poor children were given breakfast before they went to school, and where, she told her relatives, she had to wear a long rubber skirt as a protection against lice (the hall too is still there, but used by local Scouts). She also held meetings of mothers, conferences and courses, and started a painting class. She even told a friend that she had taken up painting again herself and had nearly finished a picture of Our Lord in the tomb with two angels watching. But though she obviously sympathised with the dockers and their families, she had no time for 'our dreadful strike', the Dock Strike of 1912. She told her step-daughter in Denmark:

'I think it is only the beginning of a sort of mob rule, of terrorism and revolution which is the natural outcome of the Socialistic spirit which is everywhere now.'

Journal of Journey & Stay in
Paris in Sept 1914

Started from Waterloo 10.30 P.M. Sept 4".
Only decided to go that morning; rushed about
getting Passport — Ticket etc. For my Passport it
was necessary to produce my papers of Naturalization
Went to my lawyers for these; He — Mr Witham
said it was madness to go, — that Paris would be
in the hands of the Germans in a few days —
that it would be burned & devastated just
like the Belgium towns. He added "But
its no use my talking, — I know you". This
gave me a new view of my character, which
was not flattering! While waiting at the
Home Office for my Passport I got into conversation
with a clerical gentleman, also waiting. He
was the English Chaplain of Ostend, & was
going there. He said he had, I think, a brother
there who wrote of the arrival there of the
Russian troops who had been landed in Scotland.
I expressed my doubts about it being more
than a rumour. He said "Oh don't you know, —
the N.E. railway has been closed to passengers
for some days, while they conveyed the Russians
down to London — it is an absolute fact."
So I began to believe it again — but since,
my faith in the story has relapsed.
— Arrived at Southampton about midnight.
Heard we were not to start till 4 A.M. —

The first page of Edith's Journal of her visit
to France in September 1914.

8. The Great War

However much Edith disliked Socialism, she was even more appalled at the prospect of war. In the summer of 1914 she went to the Daughters of the Heart of Mary General House in Paris to make her retreat, but by the time she returned to Rotherhithe early in August war was inevitable.

> 'In the quiet security that comes from years of peace,' she wrote to Ebba a few days later, 'I never believed in the possibility of this awful war. Alas it has come, and God alone knows when and how it will end.' And she concluded the letter: 'I am hoping, if Germany gets her deserts, Slesvig-Holstein may once more belong to Denmark. But alas – before that could come, what frightful carnage of human life there must be.'

On 3 September she wrote in an even more pessimistic mood:

> 'I feel so heart-broken over this awful war. I don't feel to have any spirit for writing. Poor Belgium a smoking devastated ruin – and now Paris invested – and I suppose she will soon be battered into ruin. Nothing seems able to stand against these ruthless barbarians. What will be the end?'

Yet the very next day she set off for Paris. For a lady of sixty-eight, who had recently told her step-daughter, 'I am really an old woman now', the next month was one of the most extraordinary, even in her life. Fortunately she kept a *Journal*, an extended diary covering fifty-three pages of an old exercise book, in which she wrote whenever she had a moment to spare. Equally fortunately, thanks to Ebba's family, the *Journal* has survived and provides a vivid record of the chaos and confusion at the time of the decisive Battle of the Marne in September 1914.

She started from Waterloo at 10.30 p.m. on Friday, 4 September. She had only decided to go that morning after receiving a telegram from the Daughters of the Heart of Mary in Paris inviting her to come and help, and so had 'rushed about getting passport, tickets etc'. Her solicitor tried to dissuade her, saying it was madness to go, but adding: 'It is no use my talking. I know you'. Edith's comment was characteristic: 'This gave me a new view of my character, which was not flattering.' Still, she got to Southampton without any trouble, crossed the Channel to Le Havre and boarded a train for Paris in the company of 'an English gentleman and the *Daily Mail* correspondent'. The journey, however, soon became a nightmare:

> 'The train was pretty empty. We started about mid-day and were told we might reach Paris about 8.30. At Rouen where there is generally a quarter of an hour stop, we all got out. I wanted to fill my little bottle

of tea, of which the milk had gone sour, with coffee. The gentlemen got out first from the restaurant and I heard them shout, "Madame - come quick", which I did, but only just in time to see the train moving quickly and the two gentlemen climbing up desperately. I was left behind!! There was my little all of luggage [in the train]! There were my provisions! I had hardly taken anything since morning tea at 6 a.m. on the boat because I expected a long day's journey. So at mid-day I had eaten one little sandwich only - and there were lovely sandwiches and Hattie's cakes and some bananas all sailing away without me to Paris!!'

Eventually she got a later train from another station. But her troubles were not over:

'I had not had time in Rouen to buy any food and now qualms of emptiness invaded my "tum tum"! I wandered along the corridor and at last found a poor man at the end cutting goodly slices from a yard-long loaf. I approached and humbly asked if he would sell me a slice. "Oh certainly, take as much as you want; take my knife" (it was very greasy but I took it gratefully and cut myself a modest slice). "Here are some sardines, cheese. Take some, lady." Wasn't it good of him, for they were his provisions for days probably. We got quite friends. I could have hugged him, poor fellow. Then I retired with my slice of bread; I had the greatest difficulty in getting him to take fifty centimes for it.'

At last a little after midnight she reached Paris. A kind porter found her a good hotel and she 'slept profoundly'. The next morning, a Sunday, she got up early and went to Mass. 'Alas,' she recorded, 'everyone seemed to be in mourning. The streets were so quiet and solitary, so unlike the usual Paris'. She collected her luggage which the gentlemen had left at the station for her and established herself at the Daughters of the Heart of Mary house in the Rue Notre Dame des Champs.

She soon realised the danger she was in:

'The Germans are awfully near. We believe we can hear the cannonading at times. Everyone is very quiet; there is no sense of panic. The churches are crowded and many look as if they were praying as they walk in the street.'

She then tried to carry out her main object in coming to France: to help soldiers wounded in the great battle that was being fought along the River Marne which would decide the fate of Paris and of France itself. But she found it 'very difficult' either to 'get an introduction to an ambulance' or even to come across any wounded. To occupy her time usefully she visited 'an ouvoir for poor women. I told them stories and tried to divert their thoughts, but they were quietly crying; some of them as they

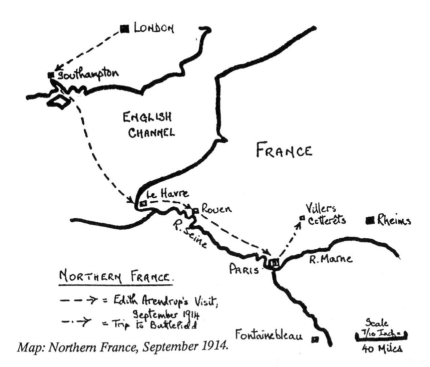

Map: Northern France, September 1914.

worked. Then I told them that my husband had been killed at the head of his men and that drew us very close together'.

At last, on 15 September after over a week's search, she had her first success:

> 'I have gained a footing in the big military hospital, Val de Grâce. There are three Englishmen and one Irishman there.' She persuaded the Commandant to let her take cigarettes and newspapers to the wounded. 'But oh dear, how bad some of the poor fellows are – such frightful wounds.'

The next day she was invited by a French priest 'to accompany him in an automobile to the "champs de guerre" to carry back wounded'. She commented:

> 'It will take a whole day to get there because the roads are so bad and the bridges blown up. It will be very terrible to see a real battlefield, but very interesting. He says I can be of real use in translating, as we are most likely to find English as well as French. I've just been to the "Bon Marcheé" to buy a Croix Rouge costume, which it seems is necessary and also some warm things as it will be very cold driving.'

The Abbé's scheme, however, came to nothing. Then three days later, 19 September, she was invited by a lady friend to go with her and a doctor in two cars 'to the "ligne de feu" to bring back wounded. We will have to ride outside with the chauffeurs coming back, as the insides will be filled with our wounded.' The next day they set out and it proved 'an unforgettable day'.

They left Paris about mid-day and reached Villers Cotterêts, about seventy kilometres to the north-west. There they saw a lot of wounded being sent off by train:

> 'So we went on further, meeting line upon line of huge motor ambulances filled with wounded and many sad groups of those who could walk. They were dragging along so wearily. But as our business was to take those who couldn't walk, we had to pass them all by, alas. At last, after passing through a forest, we came out on a high open sort of plain – once fields of corn, now a trodden mass of sludge in which the trampled sheaves mixed in with broken wheels and scattered motors; they had belonged to the Germans who had burned them before leaving them in their flight. Here we were within only about one and a half miles of the firing line. The roar of the cannon and the crackling of the bursting shells was tremendous and incessant, but nobody seemed to take any notice of it. Now at last we got our wounded – six, all we could carry. Two in one car, stretched on mattresses; four seated with pillows to support them inside the other.'

The return to Paris was eventful. The driver had not expected to be out so late and so had only brought enough acetyline for one of the car's lamps for an hour or so. In addition, while the centre of the road was good, the rest was 'slush'. In the dark forest they had to give way to an officer's car with its lamp blazing. Inevitably they got stuck in the slush and had to flag down the following car to help them out. To add to their worries, they were constantly stopped by French patrols who demanded a pass-word which they could not give. The soldiers became very suspicious:

> 'We implored them to come nearer and look at our papers. So they would gradually advance with their guns held ready. It was so funny to see their faces by the light of the lamps so fierce and ferocious gradually change to a broad smile and a good-natured "Bon Soir" as they found they were all right.'

By the time they finally reached the hospital in Paris - 2.30 a.m. the next morning - 'our poor wounded were tired out'. Edith washed them and helped get them into bed. 'They hadn't had their clothes off since the war began.' Only then could she herself go off to her bed, with one final comment: 'Oh! it is something never to be forgotten that awful glimpse of war "de près" - and even then we saw no dead lying about.'

For the rest of her stay in Paris, she never succeeded in getting so near the front again. She tried to get to Rheims, where, she had been horrified to hear, the Cathedral had been destroyed, 'an act of pure malice and hatred such as no previous wars can show a parallel'. She wanted to find out what had happened to the

44

Daughters of the Heart of Mary there as they were under constant shell-fire. 'I'm sure I could have got in all right,' she commented. 'But they [the authorities] wouldn't hear of it.' So she had to spend her time 'sorting the bundles of garments stripped from our poor wounded' or helping in 'the Ambulance', which must have been a military hospital.

> 'I go there at 6.30 a.m. after Mass and take the morning wash.' Then after bed-making and sweeping the ward, 'in the afternoon I go in sometimes to chat with them or play drafts or dominoes etc. - at which I am always beaten!'

Finally, on 6 October after just a month in France, she decided to return to England. 'If only I had studied and got my diploma [in nursing], I would have liked to stay on and worked in the Ambulance, but as it is I can do so little. And my hope of being of use to our English wounded is knocked on the head by the impossibility of getting into the ambulances.' So the next day she said good-bye to all the soldiers in her ward. 'I brought them some pears as a farewell!!'

She set off for home after going to Benediction and Night Prayers at Notre Dame. She felt Paris was now safe, but feared lest 'the judgment of God will fall upon France,' after its anti-clerical government had banned the distribution to soldiers of crosses, medals and prayer books. Her journey to England was far less eventful than the earlier one to France. There was, however, 'a very shady-looking German among the passengers. I glared at him!!' Her arrival 'home', probably the house at Rother-hithe, 'took everyone by surprise, as my postcard dated four days before has never arrived'. On this very modern note the *Journal* comes to an end.

Edith seems to have spent the rest of the war working in Rotherhithe. In her letters she talks of going to Ireland in 1916 for a holiday – 'that is if they don't take to rebellion again there' – and hopes 'to go to Paris soon for a little while', probably for her retreat. She would have liked to revisit Madeira or neutral Denmark to see Ebba and her family, but the journey was too risky because of the U-boats and 'so many charities would lose by my death'. At Rotherhithe in fact she was in danger – from Zeppelins, whose raids, she told her friend Mary Jane Wilson, were now 'far worse'. Bombs fell only two streets away from the house and the noise of 'our guns' was 'appalling'. In other ways, however, conditions round her had improved with 'less poverty than usual. So many of the husbands have gone to the War and their families get regular pay'. But she was still kept 'frightfully busy', arranging 'children's treats etc.' and, she adds: 'I have all on me, now that Miss Bayliss [another Daughter of the Heart of Mary who had been helping her] is gone.'

Despite all the work, however, the hated spectre of war was never far from her thoughts. 'Oh dearest Lord', she wrote to Mary Jane in March 1916, 'when will you end this awful scourge?' 'The horrible doings of the Germans', especially the use of gas and the sinking of the "Lusitania", appalled her. 'How awful it all is. Will there ever again be peace and friendliness? Now there seems nothing but burning hate.' But later she adds: 'Does it not seem like a sweet dream, the life before this awful war?' For a time her spirits were raised by 'the grand push', the start of the battle of the Somme. She asked Ebba: 'Are you not proud of our English troops, the "miserable little army" Germany disdained at the beginning!' But her hopes were soon dashed and at the start of November 1916 she wrote to Mary Jane: 'God help our poor soldiers through another winter'. The very next day she heard that Mary had in fact died several months earlier in Madeira and at once wrote to the Bishop of Funchal: 'I am deeply grieved at the death of Miss Wilson. She was an old and revered friend.'

The last page of Edith's Journal of her visit to France in September 1914.

9. Retirement And Death

Edith Arendrup continued working among the poor for another seven years after the end of the Great War. Very little, however, is known of her life at this time. She translated three French religious books for Burns and Oates; the last, *A Carmelite of the Sacred Heart, Marie Mercier,* came out in 1923. She may also have visited Rome, as an undated letter to Ebba from the Hotel Victoria was probably written in the early 1920s, and shows that as usual she 'scarcely had time to breathe'. Otherwise no letters to her step-daughters are available from this period.

Then in October 1925, at the age of seventy-nine, she decided it was time to retire. She had already fixed on the ideal retirement home: her old house at Bocking Bridge, Braintree. It was now a school and orphanage, run by Franciscan nuns to whom she had sold the property years before for a very 'reasonable' sum. Now she came back as an honoured guest. She was given her old room overlooking the bridge and the mill, and spent many hours in the chapel. In a letter to Ebba, written in March 1929, she showed complete contentment:

> 'I am most cosy and warm and well looked after here – and the whole house is warmed by hot pipes, and I have a delightful gas fire in my room besides.'

Edith's room in her old home, now a Convent, where she died in 1934.

Edith, now an old lady, with her dog, about the time she retired.

Mary Jane Wilson with some of her pupils in Madeira.

She still managed to go up to London twice a month to take part in meetings at the Daughters of the Heart of Mary house in Kensington. She used what she first called 'a large electric bus' and later corrected to 'motor coach', which passed the door of the Convent and went all the way to Liverpool Street. It was 'very comfortable and warm with great rugs for each person, going through very pretty country and taking about the same time as the train – and a great deal cheaper. It is like a first-class railway carriage.' From London she occasionally went down to Wimbledon to see Harriet, her children and now her grand-children. These step grand-children and step great-grand-children of Edith's knew her as 'Bedste' (pronounced Bester), short for Danish 'Bedstemor' (grandmother). They remember her as 'a commanding old lady, though not an alarming one, dressed all in black' and as 'a tall, impressive person whom the children liked because she talked to the young and brought nice presents'.

Her kindness was not confined to her relatives. She heard that the Catholics at Halstead, a small town about six miles north of Braintree, had no church and so were having to walk all the way to Braintree for Mass on Sundays. So in 1928 she bought a plot of land there large enough for a church, school and presbytery. She also paid for a small church hall to be put up as a temporary Mass centre until a proper church could be built. It was opened in September that year by the Bishop of Brentwood and, like the small chapel at Cottenham Park, soon became the focus of a growing Catholic parish. A fine modern church was later built (by her cousin, Dr. Richard Minton Courtauld), but the hall still survives and very appropriately on its end wall there hangs Edith's massive painting of a milking scene in Madeira, which used to dominate the Grensides' drawing-room in Wimbledon.

In the early 1930s she suffered yet further personal loss with the deaths of Ebba's husband, Albert, and Hattie and her husband Charles. Then her own health at last began to fail. She had an attack of bronchitis and told the Bishop of Funchal: 'I am now so old that I only write letters which are absolutely necessary.' She felt unable to attend the much delayed consecration of 'her' church of the Sacred Heart, Wimbledon, in May 1931, but received a telegram of greetings from the Bishop. Her reply, in a shaky hand, survives among the Southwark Archives: 'Thank you so much for your kind telegram. I need not say how much I value it.' It was her last direct contact with the church she had built. In December 1933 she was said to be getting weaker and resting in bed. On New Year's Day 1934 she had a major stroke and was anointed by the Convent chaplain. She was visited by Mrs. Teresa Begge, the Vice-Provincial of the Daughters of the Heart of Mary, but never regained consciousness and died on 10 January just after mid-day.

Her funeral took place two days later. Four priests officiated, including the Jesuit Rector from Wimbledon, Fr. Withnell, and she was buried by special permission near the nuns' cemetery in the grounds of the Convent overlooking the river Blackwater. The Convent archivist reported that 'the Courtaulds were nearly all present and all were much impressed with the ceremony'. Later they had a stained glass window of the Good Shepherd placed in the Convent chapel in her memory.

Edith's grave in the grounds of the Convent.

Conclusion. - A Woman Of Prayer

After her death many tributes were paid to Edith Arendrup. A friend who had known her for over forty years wrote to the *Wimbledon Borough News*:

'She was notable in many ways – great artistic talents; a skilled horsewoman, but the most notable were her absolute unselfishness, deep and tender sympathy for all who were suffering and a manner of impressive graciousness and dignity. To the Catholics of the '80s and '90s she was emphatically the great lady of Wimbledon.'

The obituary writer in *The Tablet* described her as 'a noteworthy benefactress of the Catholic revival'. He explained how she had lived well below her 'standard of income' to enable her to make her 'Catholic foundations'. Above all, he stressed her piety and reticence. 'She would have been horror-struck at the notion of an obituary.' This self-effacement so concealed the full story of her life and the true greatness of her character that within a short time of her death she was remembered only by her relatives, her fellow Daughters of the Heart of Mary and a few old friends. In 1976 mention of her name during a talk in the Sacred Heart Church Parish Hall, Wimbledon, brought blank looks from the audience. It was only the celebration of the parish centenary the following year that made her name widely known again and inspired a mothers' guild to place on the wall of the south aisle a fine memorial tablet, designed by Raymond Wells, bearing the inscription:

'It was through her Christian vision that this parish of the Sacred Heart came into being; it was through her generosity the church was built.'

A full realisation of her true greatness, however, had to wait another ten years until the centenary of the church was celebrated in 1987. The contact then established with her step great-granddaughter, Dame Gillian Brown, produced an entirely new perspective on her life, her intimate letters to her step-daughters. They show her love of children, her affectionate, un-stuffy nature, her constant concern for others – and infuriating silence on her own work, her great generosity and her love for her own country. As Dame Gillian has pointed out, 'she was rigorous to herself and did not hesitate to criticise others who were less so'. But her step-daughters were clearly devoted to her, despite her criticisms, as is proved by the fact that they kept all her letters and that their descendants still treasure them.

In the letters she rarely brings in religion. But in writing to Ebba when she was a school-girl at Cheltenham, she once added a P.S.:

'Darling – do you keep to the practice of prayer? Last night I read something about prayer which I thought you would like. Here it is:

"To pray is to raise our hearts to God, to communicate with him familiarly, though with great respect, regarding all our affairs - to confide in him; to open our hearts to Him and pour it out as it were before Him; to speak to Him of our labours, of our sins, our desires, our projects and all that occupies our minds; finally to seek in Him our consolation and our repose as one friend with another in whom he has full confidence.""

She then adds herself: 'This is not the idea of prayer that many people have, who practise it as a somewhat dry little ceremony to be performed morning and night – but I think it is the true and the wisest and highest idea of prayer – the prayer which includes all one's daily life – and enables one to make to God offerings of the smallest things; that is true prayer.'

This postscript was clearly Edith Arendrup's 'idea of prayer', the source of her spiritual life. It was constant prayer that enabled her to overcome tragedy after tragedy and led her to dedicate her life to the carrying out of God's will, no matter what it cost her. The writer in *The Tablet* described her as 'absorbed in prayer and good works'. The good works were almost unique for a lady of her background; they included the creation of three flourishing Catholic parishes and work among the poor in at least three deprived districts. But none of these 'works' would have been possible without her constant union with God. Above all else she was a woman of prayer. It was this outstanding characteristic that made Edith a truly great Victorian Catholic.

SOURCES

Letters: *Courtauld Family Letters, Vol.VIII,*(edited by S.A.Courtauld), Cambridge, 1916.
Letters of Edith Arendrup:
to Step-daughters (Owned by Arendrup family and Grenside descendants),
to Mary Jane Wilson (Owned by Franciscan Sisters, Madeira),
to Jesuit Provincial (Farm Street Archives - Wimbledon),
to Bishop of Southwark (Southwark Archives - Wimbledon).

Periodicals: *Chelmsford Chronicle*, 8 April, 1870 (Inquest on Julien Courtauld).
The Times, 13 December, 1875; 12 February, 1876 (Death of Col. Arendrup).
Surrey Independent, 31 March, 1883 (Marriage of Harriet Arendrup).
Wimbledon Borough News, 26 January, 1934 (Letter about Edith)
The Tablet, 30 January, 1934 (Obituary of Edith).
Messenger, 1934 (Appreciation of Edith).

Other Records: Marriage Certificate, Marylebone Registry Office, August 1873.
Report on the 'Affair of Gundet' by Major Dennison, 1875
Wimbledon Census Returns, 1881
Annals of the Daughters of the Heart of Mary, Vol.V, 1894-1929.
Archives of Franciscan Convent, Braintree.
Journal of a Journey and Stay in Paris, September, 1914 (Owned by the Arendrup family).

Books: On Courtaulds:
D.C. Coleman, *The Courtaulds, Vol.I*, Oxford, 1969
S.L. Courtauld *The Huguenot Family of Courtauld, Vol.III*, Private, 1967
On Artists:
E. Clayton, *English Female Artists, Vol.II*, London, 1876
A. Graves, Royal Academy, *Dictionary of Contributors, Vol.I*, London 1905

Books (cont.) B. Hiller, St.John's Wood Clique (in *Apollo*, June, 1964)
C. Wood, *Dictionary of Victorian Painters*, London, 1988
On Col. Arendrup:
Danish Biographical Dictionary, Vol.I, 1933
H.G. Marcus, *Life and Times of Menelik II*, Oxford, 1975
On France:
R. Price, *Social History of Nineteenth Century France*,
London, 1980
On Friends:
T. Dunphy, *Invincible Victorian: Life of Mary Jane
Wilson*, (no date)
Fr.J. Pollen, *Life and Letters of Fr. John Morris, S.J.*,
London, 1896
On Wimbledon:
Birth of a Mission, London, 1926
R.J. Milward, *Portrait of a Parish*, London, 1977
R.J. Milward, *Portrait of a Church*, London, 1987